VIC THE VET

"I just put it down on my VA Supplies Form"

VIC THE VET

by GABE JOSEPHSON

ABOUT COMICS | Camarillo, California

Vic the Vet by Gabe Josephson.

Original edition published by Syracuse University Press, 1947.

Introduction and annotations by Nat Gertler
© 2016 About Comics.

This edition published by About Comics, Camarillo, California.
ISBN-13: 978-1936404-65-0

Continuous printing starting September, 2016.

Address all inquiries to *questions@aboutcomics.com*. Direct wholesale orders
and custom cover editions are available.

INTRODUCTION

After their successful completion of World War II, American servicemen took their discharges from the armed forces and flooded American campuses, underwritten by new veteran benefits. Purple Heart recipient and Battle of the Bulge fighter Gabriel Josephson was among this new batch of freshmen. He landed himself at Syracuse University, a central New York institution that took on more of these men fresh out of uniform (or, in some cases, still wearing their uniforms) than any other school in the state.

In 1946 Gabe started drawing "Vic the Vet," a single-panel cartoon that ran in the campus paper, the *Syracuse Daily Orange*. In that strip, he found plenty of humor in how he and others were faring in making that military-to-academia transition, as well as taking his shots at the fashions of the day, the battle of the sexes, and campus life in general. In 1947, Syracuse University Press published a book collection of those cartoon while new installments were still appearing; this book reprints that book with added annotations and two additional cartoons. (The captions have been re-typeset for clarity.)

Doing the cartoons was not a distraction from the pursuit of a career but rather a part of it. Gabe, who was an illustration major, would be a cartoonist and a book illustrator in the years after his graduation in 1950. His freelance clients included Walt Disney Productions, the *New York Times Book Review,* and *Sesame Street*.

Mr. Josephson is no longer with us, but his cartoons remain to give us a wonderful picture of a unique period.

–Nat Gertler
September, 2016

It was a hot summer day in 1946 when Vic the Vet made a collegiate entrance into Syracuse University. He pulled his convertible into a parking space next to a fire-plug, pointed proudly to his car and boasted, "I got it on my veteran's supply form." It was a hotter day when he entered his French 10a class with a chocolate bar in his hand.

College life has done a lot for Vic. Instead of being readjusted, he is now maladjusted. He recently strolled by a recruiting office and laughed and laughed and laughed at the enlistment poster outside. The recruiting officer moaned, "He's ruining our business."

Vic looks at college life through the eyes of his creator, Gabe Josephson. Some people say that Vic looks like Gabe. He does.

And Gabe's troubles make the woes of Vic the Vet look like picayune problems. Four semesters at Syracuse find Gabe still a frosh, not through choice, nor scholastic ineptness. Gabe has switched colleges three times. Each time he's started over. It will take Gabe and Vic five years to get a diploma and then Vic will probably go out and earn Gabe a living.

Gabe's creative genius is not confined to Vic alone. The Josephson girl is a Syracuse coed, her body camouflaged by blue jeans, her intelligence, if any, masked behind slant eyed bifocals. The Josephson professor is the college prof who accentuates the faults found in any faculty, ranging from the pot bellied, spectacled old timer, to the eager fauntleroyed young instructor. Gabe's veteran wears his ruptured duck on his tux and owns enough GI clothing to drive a supply sergeant to suicide.

Gabe's troubles are Vic's troubles. Vic's troubles are the average veteran's troubles on campus. With a high number in the housing draw he innocently demands Chancellor Tolley's residence. Needing credits for graduation he demands of the registrar, "How much credit for the three years' latrine orderly?" Surrounded by armed guards, barbed wire and a baggypantsed proctor with a .45, he inquires, "Is this exam on the honor system?"

Gabe has his serious side. During the recent campaign for alleviation of traffic ills on the Hill, he bluntly asked the city to "Take the Blinders Off." As OPA was lifted he showed the G.I. student going through the wringer as inflation with its high room rent, high cost of food, and threatened tuition rises pressed him.

Through semesters Vic has mirrored the veteran on campus, often cynically, often bitterly, but always with a big dash of humor and a big dash of originality. He hired a P.W. to carry his books, used a walkie talkie to beat the exams, automatically stooped to pick up cigarette butts, stood in a dispensary line waiting for a physical clad in nothing but a GI raincoat, and met Sad Sack in a dining hall line, and queried, "Haven't I seen you someplace before?"

Vic doesn't like uniforms. An ROTC student showed his ribbons to Vic. "I got this for no cuts in ROTC." He saw a pfc. in ill-fitting khakis. "He's in ASTP. He never got his shipping orders."

Vic has women trouble. "Another New Year's eve resolution shot to hell," he moaned after a Hill coed blackened his eye. And two coeds coming out of a rest room asked him, "Isn't there anyplace this guy Kilroy hasn't been?"

Vic and Gabe will be around for quite a while yet. And as the team ages, it mellows, and blends with the times as skirts grow longer, beers get shorter, and veterans still sweat out checks.

"What do they do for
extra curricular activities around here?"

Vic is seen throughout this volume wearing the *Honorable Service Lapel Button*. Nicknamed "the ruptured duck", this badge was given to folks honorably discharged from the U.S. military from 1939 through 1946. Veterans were permitted to wear their uniform with this pinned to the lapel or with a cloth version stitched on, circumventing laws prohibiting the wearing of military uniforms by those not currently in active service. This permission proved convenient, given the clothing shortages of the day. Many vets continued to wear the pin on their civilian clothes as a sign of their service.

Previous page:

Servicemen stationed in France found a country of desperate shortages where their standard ration items like cigarettes and chocolate bars proved to be powerful currency, particularly for prostitution.

Next page:

The *Army Specialized Training Program* (or *ASTP*) began during World War II to train men in technical skills and prepare them as junior officers. While the goal was to give them four years of training in an 18 month period, many participants found their enrollment cut short as the demand for manpower on the battlefield and were sent off to combat.

"He's left over from A.S.T.P.
They lost his shipping orders."

"You mean this ain't like the ones
we used to get in the army?"

"Boy, am I glad to be out of the army.
I always felt like a fool in those silly clothes."

"I understand they had to take him.
He used to be in the K-9 corps."

"I understand that applied science is a snap."

Next page:

The GI Bill of Rights, which provided veterans with funding for college, included subsistence payments to cover the veteran's general life needs. Students were not eligible for these *subsistence checks* until they had been enrolled for thirty days, but despite official attempts to control the lag, first payments often faced considerable delays.

"Has my first subsistence check come yet?"

He sneaked him back in his duffle bag.

Previous page:

Foreign soldiers held as prisoners of war by American forces were given American uniforms with *P.W.* painted on them for easy identification.

Many young instructors were added to the staff.
"That's Dr. Smith. He took the accelerated course."

"They must'a found a mistake on his discharge."

"Oh, he knows his stuff.
He just doesn't know how to teach it."

"You know a better way?"

"Haven't I seen you somewhere before?"

Previous page:

Former Disney animator Sergeant George Baker's pantomime comics series **The Sad Sack** first appeared in **Yank, The Army Weekly** in 1942. The popular title character would go on to star in feature films and comic books.

"No coffee, please. I have an afternoon class
and it might keep me awake."

Next page:
Soldiers charged with *policing* an area (clearing away debris and trash) frequently found that most of their effort was clearing away cigarette butts tossed by their fellow servicemen.

"Poor Hobbs, he was in France too long."

"...and then I said to the director of housing,
'you can't do this to me.'"

"... and this one's for not cutting any classes for two months."

"He said something about, 'It writes
for 98 years without refilling.' "

"How much farther can this inflation go?"

"Able One to Red Dog. . . . what's the base
angle of an isosceles circle?   . . .Over."

"Gee, just like the separation center."

"He says he wants eight hours of classes a day so he can be sure of getting his eight hours sleep."

"You're taking too broad a view
of the G.I. Bill of Rights."

Previous page:

The *Servicemen's Readjustment Act of 1944*, more frequently called the *G.I. Bill of Rights* or simply the *G.I. Bill*, guaranteed returning veterans who had served at least four months a free college or technical education, low-cost loans for houses or businesses, and unemployment compensation. It did, however, have its limits.

(Folks looking for Josephson's artistic influences should note the Dr. Seussishness of the female captive.)

41

"How did you know we are roommates?"

"Well, do something. He's ruining our business."

"Oh, don't be so eager."

"Take a good look around.
I think we're paying for the atmosphere."

"Just where did you say you were separated from?"

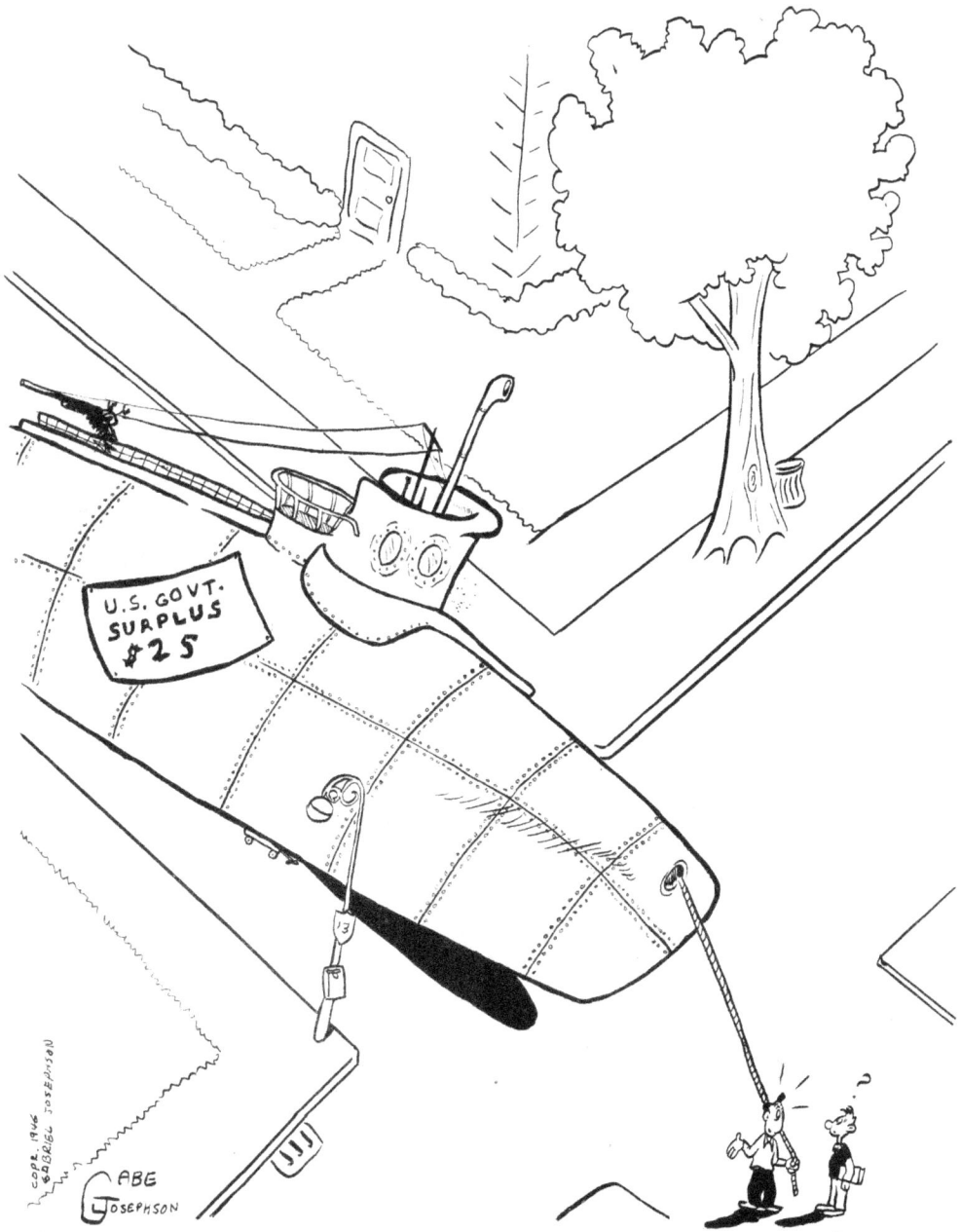

"... yeah, I know. But what a bargain it was!"

"I understand it was the only way he could
get any answers out of them."

**As the Colgate game drew near they caught
him using THAT tooth paste.**

Previous page:

The raucously celebrated college football rivalry between Syracuse University and nearby Colgate University ran from 1891 to 1961, during which the teams played each other 62 times. The two teams have played each other a mere handful of times in the last half century.

"I don't care how hard it's snowing,
take it out where it belongs."

"Why doesn't that guy forget he was a captain?"

"This is a pretty good course in sidewalk engineering."

"Oh, well . . . another New Year's resolution
shot to Hell."

"Been window shopping again?"

"It looks like I'll major in prerequisites again."

"Combat nothing—registration."

Next page:

In 1948, the year after this cartoon ran, what had been Syracuse University's New York College of Forestry got subsumed into the newly-formed State University of New York. Today, it is called State University of New York College of Environmental Science and Forestry (SUNY-ESF), and its students are still allowed to take classes at Syracuse.

"The lectures ain't so bad—it's the homework."

"How did you know I used to be an officer?"

"You can't pass everything."

"He wants to know how much credit for three
years as a latrine orderly?"

"You're catching on. One or two more times
and you'll have it."

"He's the fastest waiter in here."

All campus eating places are to be kept clean.
"There's lipstick on this glass."

Next page:
Campusing is a method of discipline where the student is restricted to campus.

"Campused again?"

"Tough exam?"

"What parking problem?"

Next page:

The phrase *KILROY WAS HERE*, generally accompanied by a drawing of a bald guy peeking over a wall, was a popular piece of graffiti in the World War II era, appearing in many an unlikely spot.

"Isn't there anyplace that Kilroy hasn't been?"

"Once a supply sergeant,
always a supply sergeant."

"One more word about 'it's raining violets,' and I'll shove a fist down your throat."

Previous page:
"It's raining violets" is a lyric from the song "April Showers," which was written in 1921 and first popularized by Al Jolson. The song has been covered many times; around the time of this cartoon, a Frank Sinatra rendition could be heard on the radio, and Guy Lombardo & His Royal Canadians released their version.

Next page:
The first day of the month was when the veterans' subsistence checks were scheduled to arrive.

"You can always tell when the first of the
month rolls around."

"The crew's shaping up pretty well under the new coach."

FINE ARTS ↓   ACCOUNTING ↓   JOURNALISM ↓

GABE JOSEPHSON

Registration is well planned now.

"He wants to know what's the other one's name."

"All I said was, 'Drop dead!'"

The coeds blossomed out.

"... and now for today's demonstration on electricity!"

"I wonder how she'd look in a bathing suit?"

"Don't you think short skirts were more immoral?"

"There goes another bow-legged one."

Next page:
"The D.O." would be the *Syracuse Daily Orange,* the campus newspaper in which these cartoons originally appeared.

"I know you work on the D.O. but let's not
carry freedom of the press too far."

"It's those little friendly rivalries that
add so much to college life."

Wadaya mean, term paper! . . . V.A. forms! _ _

Previous page:

The "V.A." was the Veterans Administration, the government agency charged with handling the benefits due to U.S. veterans. It has since been superseded by the United States Department of Veterans Affairs.

"Is that what you mean by 'short skirt'?"

"He's been that way ever since he got that
bottle for Christmas."

"At least they can't say, 'your slip is showing' anymore."

"I gotta dress like this to get into football games.
They put the wrong picture in my passbook."

"I'll have you knew we write the news as we see it!"

Next page:

During World War I, the U.S. Food Administration (the government agency charged with providing food supplies for the military) called on Americans to observe "meatless Mondays" and "wheatless Wednesdays" to reduce consumption of those items and leave more for the troops.

"... Ah, foodless Wednesday."

"No he's not reading the comics—it's the fashion page."

"This pencil feeds new leads like a machine gun."

"But Mace Cottage Open House only has cider,
while Heffron Cottage has ginger snaps."

"He's finishing an unfinished fifth."

"Is this test on the honor system?

Next page:

This final cartoon did not appear in the original 1947 edition of this book. You can tell that the book was already out before this cartoon was published, because one of the characters in the cartoon is actually reading a copy!

"New Look, Hell . . . It's the Same Old Look!"

For more Gabe Josephson cartoons, get

ADULT
COLORING
BOOKS
OF THE
1960s

Reprinting eleven classic
satirical coloring books,
including Gabe's
The Skier's Coloring Book!

Published by About Comics.

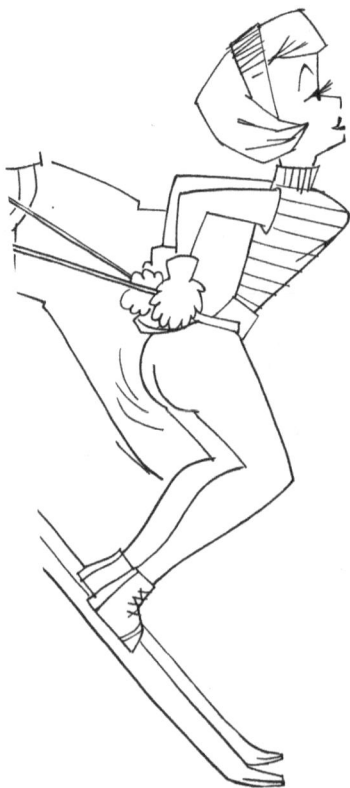

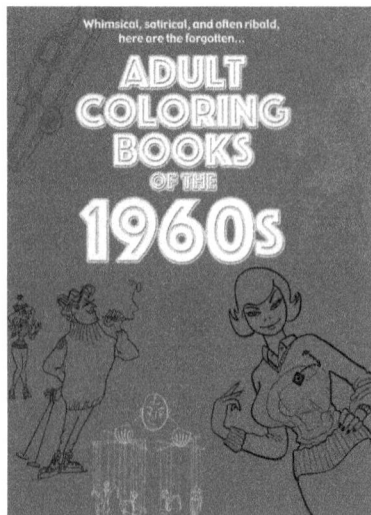

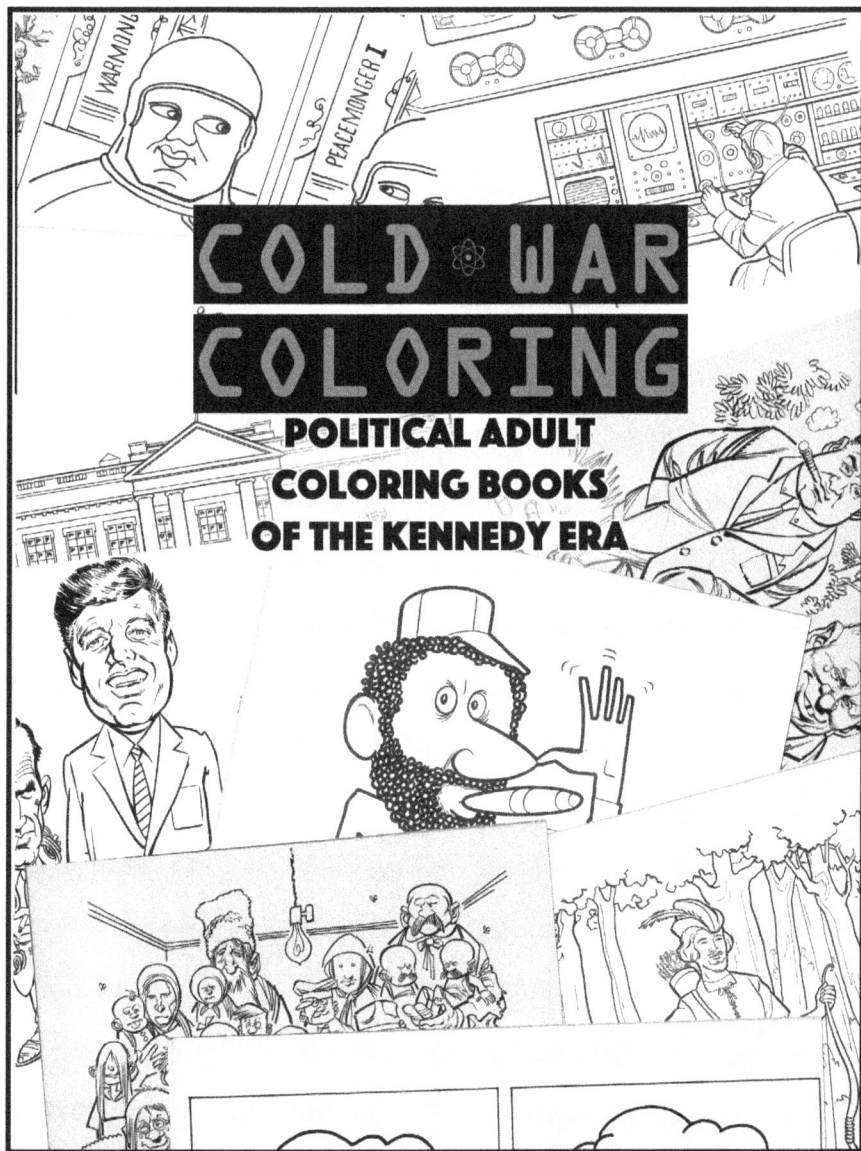

COLD☢WAR COLORING

POLITICAL ADULT COLORING BOOKS OF THE KENNEDY ERA

Kids'
Letters to
President
Kennedy

Selected by
BILL ADLER
Illustrated by
LOUIS DARLING

For a full list of our
books of historical and
cartooning interest,
check out
AboutComics.com

Dear President
Johnson

KIDS' LETTERS TO LBJ
Selected by Bill   Illustrated by Charles M.
ADLER   SCHULZ

www.ingramcontent.com/pod-product-compliance
Lightning Source LLC
Chambersburg PA
CBHW031628040426
42452CB00007B/733